Diet recommendations during pancreatic cancer

Diet can support the affected organs and is not a treatment for the disease. Please check these recommendations always with a nutrition consultant, therapist, doctor or dietician. The recipes and the list of ingredients are supporting the conventional medical therapy. The calorie disclosures of fresh ingredients (fruit and vegetables) vary according to quality and time of harvest. The contents were checked by a dietician and a nutrition consultant for the Traditional Chinese Medicine (TCM).

Author:
©2017 Josef Miligui
www.ebns.at

AF206934

Source:
The lists are created from the EBNS database for nutritional counseling. The database is used by dietitians, therapists and doctors for advising the patient / client.

Literature:
The specialist literature and the training documents of the German and Austrian dietary and traditional Chinese medicine serve as a knowledge base. We have used the documents as a basis of knowledge, adapted it to our experience and completed them.
http://di-book.com

Title Foto:
©2008 Erika Weixlbaumer

Production and publishing:
BoD – Books on Demand, Norderstedt
ISBN: 9783746097763

Diet recommendations during pancreatic cancer

1 Treatment strategy

50-60% carbohydrates, 20% protein, 30% fat (MCT - dietary margarine, oils) Take several smaller meals (5 to 7) a day. This facilitates the work of the digestive system. Take your medication regularly. Enzyme preparations are best consumed with some liquid during each meal to allow mixing with food. Be patient if you should lose weight first. Experience has shown that it can take three months or more to increase again.

2 Avoid

Alcohol, fatty food.

3 Breakfast
kkal. per serving

4 Snack

5 Lunch

6 Afternoon

7 Dinner

8 Any time

9 Recipes

(recommendable) = You can use more.
(little) = You should use less than specified or omit.

9.1 Adzuki Bean and Rice Soup

Strengthens spleen, heart, kidney and stomach, supports urination,
improves blood circulation, reduces inflammation.
Cooking time approx. 2 hours
Calories p. portion: 199
1 portions
Allergens:

Quantity of ingredients:
Adzuki beans 8 table spoons / 40g. (recommended)
Rice round grain 2 table spoons / 20g. (recommended)
Water 1 1/2 cups / 200g. (yes)
Honey 1 table spoon / 8g. (little)

Cooking instructions:
Boil soaked adzuki beans and round grain rice in a ratio of 4: 1 in water
until a thin pulp has formed. Sweet as needed; possibly puree.

Effect: This recipe strengthens kidney, spleen and stomach and is
particularly suitable for mothers with too little milk flow.

9.2 Andalusian fish pot

Strengthens immune system, prevents cancer, dissolves stagnation,
promotes weight loss. Good to fight immunodeficiency, loss of appetite,
flatulence, high blood pressure, depressions, diabetes, diarrhea,
stimulates appetite.
Cooking time approx. 30 min
Calories p. portion: 348
4 portions
Allergens: ADLO

Quantity of ingredients:
Basic recipe for a vegetable soup 2 cups / 500g. (recommended)
Onion (spring onion) 2 pieces / 40g. (recommended)
Olive oil 1 table spoon / 20g. (recommended)
Lemon peel 1/2 piece / 3g. (yes)
Bay leaf 1 piece / 1g. (yes)

Potato 5/8 oz / 200g. (recommended)
Cod 3/4 lbs / 300g. (yes)
White wine 4 table spoons / 80g. (little)
Lemon juice 1/2 teaspoon / 10g. (yes)
Salt 1 pinch / 1g. (little)
Pepper (ground) 1 pinch / 0,2g. (yes)
Parsley 1 table spoon / 15g. (recommended)
White bread (wheat bread) 8 slices / 250g. (little)

Cooking instructions:
Boil the vegetable broth with small spring onion, olive oil, grated lemon peel and bay leaf. Boil covered for 10 minutes. Add the peeled, diced potatoes and boil in about 8 minutes. Add fish pieces and white wine and switch to small heat. In the slightly boiling broth put the fish and boil it a few minutes. Season with lemon juice, salt and pepper. Serve with parsley sprinkled.
White bread as a side dish.

9.3   Apricot Oat Balls with Acai powder

Strengthens immune system, little laxative, antioxidativ.
Cooking time approx. 20 min
Calories p. portion: 768
2 portions
Allergens: AHO

Quantity of ingredients:
Oat flakes (whole grain) 1/4 lbs - 4oz / 125g. (recommended)
Apricot dried 1/4 lbs - 4oz / 125g. (little)
Almond 1/4 lbs - 4oz / 100g. (yes)
Honey 2 table spoons / 14g. (little)
Acai powder 3 teaspoons / 9g. (recommended)
Lemon juice 2 table spoons / 9g. (yes)

Cooking instructions:
Lightly chop the sliced almonds in the pan and let them cool. Then pour the apricots in the blender and add lemon juice. Mix all the ingredients together. If the mass is too loose add some honey. Finally, form small balls and roll them in oat flakes.

9.4   Artichoke soup

Detoxifying, supports urination, regulates digestion, stimulates appetite, gentle laxative, forcing spleen, promotes weight loss. Strengthens gastrointestinal function, expands blood vessels, prevents cancer.
Cooking time approx. 40 min
Calories p. portion: 142
3 portions
Allergens: GLN

Quantity of ingredients:
Artichoke 4 pieces / 400g. (recommended)
Butter organic 1 table spoon / 20g. (little)
Onion (shallot) 1 piece / 20g. (recommended)
Corn flour 1 table spoon / 10g. (yes)
Nutmeg 1 pinch / 0,5g. (yes)
Basic recipe for a vegetable soup 1 cup / 250g. (recommended)
Salt 1 pinch / 0,5g. (little)
Lemon 1/4 piece / 8g. (yes)
Lemon peel 1/4 piece / g. (yes)
Turmeric (yellow root) 1 pinch / 1g. (recommended)
Sesame paste (Tahini) 1 table spoon / 10g. (yes)
Sesame, white 1 teaspoon / 10g. (yes)

Cooking instructions:
Boil the artichokes in 2 liters of water with salt until the outer leaves are light removable. Remove leaves and flower center (fibrous) so that only the soil remains.
Melt the butter, cut the onion into small pieces and steam gently; add some cornmeal, nutmeg; brew with vegetable soup; add salt, a little lemon peel and juice, turmeric and artichoke bottoms, cook gently and puree; Season with Tahin and sprinkle with sesame before serving.

9.5   Baked chicory

Mineral supporter and is full of A-B-C vitamins.
Cooking time approx. 20 min
Calories p. portion: 230
2 portions
Allergens: AG

Quantity of ingredients:
Chicory 4 pieces / 500g. (yes)
Cream, sweet 30% 2 table spoons / 40g. (little)
Breadcrumbs (wheat bread, bread roll) 2 table spoons / 20g. (yes)
Rice Basmati 1/2 cup / 60g. (recommended)
Water 3 cups / 300g. (yes)
Salt 1 pinch / 1g. (little)

Cooking instructions:
Blanch chicory in hot water whole for about 5 minutes; place in a casserole dish; put some sweet cream over it; put the bread crumbs over the chicory and gratinate.

Place the rice in salted water, heat till it boils and let it simmer over low heat for about 15 minutes.

9.6   Barley soup

Diuretic, forcing spleen, supports urination, stimulates liver function, antioxidativ, promotes digestion, detoxifying, reduces blood lipids, stimulates, dissolves stagnation.
Cooking time approx. 25 min
Calories p. portion: 265
2 portions
Allergens: A

Quantity of ingredients:
Barley 1 cup / 120g. (yes)
Salt 1 pinch / 1g. (little)
Ginger fresh 1/2 teaspoon / 1g. (recommended)
Olive oil 1 table spoon / 10g. (recommended)
Parsley 2 table spoons / 30g. (recommended)
Water 1 1/2 cups / 240g. (yes)

Cooking instructions:
Roast the barley in the pan, then grind it to the ground, and boil with water, some salt and ginger to a mash. Before serving add oil and parsley.

Variant: You can add a better taste to the dish if you cook it with prepared vegetable or meat broth.

9.7   Basmati rice + Zucchini tofu dish

Diuretic, supports urination, harmonizes spleen and stomach, reduces flatulence, good to fight body overweight and high blood pressure. Antioxidativ, promotes digestion, perspiration, reduces blood lipids, forcing spleen.
Cooking time approx. 20 min
Calories p. portion: 146
4 portions
Allergens: E

Quantity of ingredients:
Soy Tofu 5/8 lbs - 8oz / 250g. (yes)
Olive oil 2 table spoons / 6g. (recommended)
Coriander 1/2 teaspoon / 4g. (yes)
Ginger fresh 1/2 teaspoon / 4g. (recommended)
Rice Basmati 1/2 cup / 60g. (recommended)
Water 3 cups / 200g. (yes)
Zucchini 1 piece / 700g. (yes)

Cooking instructions:
Cut tofu cubes and marinate with olive oil, tamari, crushed coriander and ginger. Leave at least 1 hour.
Cook Basmati rice with the water. You can season with onion and cardamom.
Roast zucchini and tofu in pan in the hot oil for approx. 5-7 min.
Serve rice and tofu on a plate.
Add the parsley.
Can also be used as a salad for the home and on the go.

9.8   Bath with rosemary

Stimulating.
Cooking time approx. 10 min
Calories p. portion: 2
2 portions
Allergens:
Quantity of ingredients:
Rosemary 1 sachet / 5g. (yes)

Cooking instructions:
Put a tied bag with the rosemary in the water and let it soak for 10 minutes. The bag can be squeezed several times before removing it.

9.9 Bean paste piquant sweet

Supports urination, lowers cholesterol, prevents arteriosclerosis, antioxidativ. Promotes digestion, helps to digest fat, supports urination, reduces blood pressure.
Cooking time approx. 1 hour
Calories p. portion: 311
1 portions
Allergens: MO

Quantity of ingredients:
Black beans 1 cup / 120g. (recommended)
Ginger fresh 1 inch / 3g. (recommended)
Boxhorn clover seeds 1/2 teaspoon / 2g. (yes)
Tomato paste 1 table spoon / 10g. (recommended)
Olive oil 2 table spoons / 20g. (recommended)
Pumpkin seed oil 1 dash / 3g. (yes)
Mustard 1 knife tip / 1g. (yes)
Radish horseradish 1 teaspoon (grated) / 2g. (yes)
Pepper (ground) 1 pinch / 0,5g. (yes)
Garlic 2 cloves / 3g. (recommended)
Salt 1 pinch / 1g. (little)
Sugar molasses 2 table spoons / 20g. (little)
Lemon peel 1/2 piece / 1g. (yes)

Cooking instructions:
Boil beans (with spices and ginger), drain water and puree. Season with spices.

Refine with sugar beet syrup and lemon peel.

9.10 Bilberry - curd cheese with Acai powder

Good to fight weakness, belching, diabetes, acute or chronic obstruction of the bowel, skin problems. Laxative, antibacterial effect. Antioxidant.
Cooking time approx. 10 min
Calories p. portion: 238
2 portions
Allergens: GH

Quantity of ingredients:
Blueberry 5/8 oz / 200g. (recommended)
Orange juice 2 table spoons / 10g. (little)
Maple syrup 1 table spoon / 5g. (little)
Almond 1 table spoon / 5g. (yes)
Curd cheese 20% 5/8 lbs - 8oz / 250g. (yes)
Sugar cane sugar 1 table spoon / 9g. (little)
Acai powder 2 teaspoons / 5g. (recommended)
Cinnamon ground 1 pinch / 0,5g. (yes)

Cooking instructions:
Rinse the blueberries in a sieve and pat dry gently. Drizzle with orange juice and maple syrup and stir in the Acai powder.
Roast the almond sticks in a frying pan until golden brown until they are fragrant and allow to cool on a plate. Dust with a little cinnamon.
Stir quark and sugar until smooth.
Layer alternately the quark with the marinated blueberries in glasses and garnish with the almonds.

9.11 Black root with yogurt

Stimulates kidney, bladder and forces the cleaning of the body. In the physiological sense, they generally stimulate the glands in the organism. Good to fight acute or chronic constipation of the intestine. Rich in Vitamins and trace elements.
Cooking time approx. 20 min
Calories p. portion: 424
2 portions
Allergens: AG

Quantity of ingredients:
Salsify 1 lbs / 400g. (recommended)
Yogurt (natural, 1.5% fat) 4 table spoons / 80g. (yes)
Herbs various 1 table spoon / 8g. (yes)
Salt 1 pinch / 1g. (little)
Herbs various 2 table spoons / 6g. (yes)
Multi-grain bread (gray bread) 6 slices / 120g. (yes)

Cooking instructions:
Peel the salsify and simmer in salted water until tender. Pour away the water, cool the salsify and cut it to size. Cover with yoghurt and sprinkle with fresh herbs. Serve with the bread.
You can also use the salsify from the conserve.

9.12 Celery and potato cream soup

Reduces blood pressure, strengthens immune system, promotes weight loss. Good to fight immunodeficiency, loss of appetite, flatulence, depressions, diabetes, diarrhea, improves digestion.
Cooking time approx. 45 min
Calories p. portion: 113
4 portions
Allergens: GL

Quantity of ingredients:
Olive oil 1 table spoon / 10g. (recommended)
Onion white 1/2 piece / 25g. (yes)
Basic recipe for a vegetable soup 3 cups / 700g. (recommended)
Potato 5/8 oz / 200g. (recommended)
Nutmeg 1 pinch / 0,5g. (yes)
Ground 1 pinch / 0,5g. (yes)
Lemon peel 1/4 piece / 1g. (yes)
Créme fraiche cheese 2 table spoons / 20g. (little)
Salt 1 pinch / 1g. (little)
Parsley 1 table spoon / 8g. (recommended)

Cooking instructions:
Heat the olive oil in a saucepan lightly. Fry the onions very gently in a mild heat. Pour with vegetable stock according to the basic recipe.
Cover and cook for 15 minutes.
Add curd-cut potato, celery, nutmeg, cumin and lemon zest. Spice with salt and cook for 12 minutes. Potatoes and celery should be soft.
Remove the lemon peel.
Puree the soup with crème fraiche using a blender. Season the soup with salt.
Arrange the soup in portions with the chopped parsley.

9.13 Celery juice

Mineral and vitamin rich, forces metabolism and dehydrating effect.
Cooking time approx. 5 min
Calories p. portion: 33
1 portions
Allergens: L

Quantity of ingredients:
Celery root 1/2 piece / 200g. (recommended)
Water 1 cup / 120g. (yes)
Salt 1 pinch / 0,5g. (little)

Cooking instructions:
Peel celeriac and cut into pieces and juice. Mix with water and salt as needed.

9.14 Champignon salad with cress

Promotes digestion and is good to fight high blood pressure. Good to fight loss of appetite, improves blood circulation.
Cooking time approx. 5 min
Calories p. portion: 220
1 portions
Allergens: AN

Quantity of ingredients:
Champignon 5/8 lbs - 8oz / 250g. (yes)
Sesame oil 2 table spoons / 6g. (recommended)
Pepper (ground) 1 pinch / 0,5g. (yes)
Salt 1 pinch / 1g. (little)
Lemon 1/2 piece / 15g. (yes)
Peppers powder 2 pinches / 0,1g. (yes)
Cress 2 table spoons / 10g. (yes)
White bread (wheat bread) 2 slices / 30g. (little)

Cooking instructions:
Cut mushrooms into thin slices.
Dressing: sesame oil, a little ground pepper, salt, plenty of lemon juice, stir well the rose pepper; give over the finely chopped mushrooms; plenty of watercress.
Goes well with: white bread, round grain rice or quinoa; Along with the cereal, the salad makes a simple, light meal.
Serve with white bread.

9.15 Chickpeas with Raisins

Reduces blood pressure, strengthens immune system. Relaxes breast pressure, moisturizer dry skin, helps to fight incontinence. Strengthens spleen and stomach, strengthens the muscles.
Cooking time approx. 45 min
Calories p. portion: 429
2 portions
Allergens: EGO

Quantity of ingredients:
Chickpeas 1 cup / 120g. (yes)
Hijiki 1 table spoon / 7g. (yes)
Salt 1 pinch / 0,5g. (little)
Sunflower oil 1 table spoon / 10g. (recommended)
Carrot 2 pieces / 160g. (recommended)
Raisins 2 table spoons / 18g. (little)
Ginger fresh 1/2 teaspoon / 2g. (recommended)
Cumin (Caraway seed) 1 pinch / 0,2g. (yes)
Lemon juice 1 dash / 1g. (yes)
Sour cream 15% fat 1 table spoon / 8g. (little)
Curcuma 1 pinch / 0,2g. (recommended)
Soybean milk 1 dash / 1g. (yes)
Coriander 1 pinch / 0,2g. (yes)
Soy sauce 1 dash / 1g. (yes)
Rice round grain 1/2 cup / 60g. (recommended)
Water 3 cups / 250g. (yes)
Salt 1 pinch / 1g. (little)

Cooking instructions:
Preparation:
Soak chickpeas in cold water for several hours or overnight.

After that:
Pour soaking water away; put the chickpeas in cold water; Add 1 tbsp Hijiki and cook the chickpeas bite-proof; Add salt at the end of the cooking time.

Separately:
In a hot pan, fry oil, chopped carrots (more than chickpeas), raisins, grated ginger, plenty of cumin and salt until the carrots are half cooked; add the chickpeas and sea algae; Add lemon juice, a little sour cream, turmeric, soy or rice milk; a pinch of cilantro, add some soy sauce; Let it

soak for a few minutes over low heat until the carrots are cooked.

Put the round grain rice with the water, salt and cook for about 20 minutes.

9.16 Cranberry yogurt mix

Good to fight acute or chronic constipation of the intestine, oral mucosal inflammation, diarrhea, flatulence, throat irritation.
Cooking time approx. 5 min
Calories p. portion: 57
2 portions
Allergens: GO

Quantity of ingredients:
Yogurt (natural, 1.5% fat) 1/4 lbs - 4oz / 125g. (yes)
Cranberry jam 2 table spoons / 20g. (little)
Mineral water 1 cup / 250g. (yes)

Cooking instructions:
Mix yoghurt, cranberry jam and mineral water until frothy.

9.17 Fruit jelly

Promotes spleen and liver, reduces blood pressure, strengthens immune system. Promotes digestion. Warms stomach and spleen, improves blood circulation. For cholesterol diet.
Cooking time approx. 2 hours and more
Calories p. portion: 60
2 portions
Allergens:

Quantity of ingredients:
Carrot (Early Carrot) 3/4 lbs / 300g. (recommended)
Water 6 table spoons / 50g. (yes)
Sugar cane sugar 1 teaspoon / 3g. (little)
Gelatin white 1 Leaf / 3g. (yes)
Orange 1/2 piece / 50g. (yes)
Cinnamon ground 1 pinch / 0,2g. (yes)
Corn germ oil 1/2 teaspoon / 2g. (yes)

Cooking instructions:
Thoroughly wash, clean, peel and slice the carrots.

Boil about 6 tablespoons of water in a saucepan, add the carrots and cane sugar and cook over medium heat for 10-15 minutes.

Meanwhile, soak the gelatin in cold water for about 10 minutes.

Squeeze the orange half, mix the juice with the cinnamon and the oil. Crush the hot carrots with the blender and dissolve the gelatine (alternative: use agar-agar) in the hot mush.
Stir in the orange juice. Swirl out a pudding mold (1/4 liter content) with cold water, pour in the carrot sauce and refrigerate in the fridge for about 3 hours.
Tip out before eating and allow to warm to room temperature.

9.18 Hearty winter breakfast

Strengthens immune system, calms nerves and stomach, promotes digestion, detoxifying, strengthens bodily production, promotes perspiration, reduces blood lipids, stimulates, dissolves stagnation.
Cooking time approx. 20 min
Calories p. portion: 678
1 portions
Allergens: ACEG

Quantity of ingredients:
Oat meal 1 cup / 120g. (yes)
Ginger fresh 1/2 teaspoon / 1g. (recommended)
Salt 1 pinch / 1g. (little)
Onion (spring onion) 2 pieces / 40g. (recommended)
Chicken egg 1 piece / 55g. (yes)
Butter organic 1 table spoon / 15g. (little)
Soy sauce 1 dash / 3g. (yes)

Cooking instructions:
Soak oatmeal overnight. Boil in the morning with a little ginger, salt and a spring onion or leek and then let it swell until the porridge is soft. Before serving, add a whole egg to the porridge, add the butter and season to taste with a little soy sauce.

Recommendation: Especially suitable for the cold season.

9.19 Lentil and chestnut soup with curry

Reduces blood pressure, strengthens immune system, prevents cancer, reduces radiation damage, forcing spleen, dissolves stagnation, promotes weight loss. Good to fight immunodeficiency, loss of appetite, flatulence, high blood pressure, depressions, diabetes, diarrhea.
Cooking time approx. 45 min
Calories p. portion: 176
4 portions
Allergens: LO

Quantity of ingredients:
Lentils red 3/8 lbs - 6oz / 150g. (yes)
Chestnuts 3/8 lbs - 6oz / 150g. (recommended)
Olive oil 1 table spoon / 10g. (recommended)
Curry 2 teaspoons / 8g. (recommended)
Turmeric (yellow root) 1 teaspoon / 2g. (recommended)
Basic recipe for a vegetable soup 2 cup / 500g. (recommended)
White wine 1/2 cup / 125g. (little)
Salt (herbal) 1 pinch / 1g. (little)
Anise (Common Fennel) 1 pinch / 1g. (recommended)
Cardamom 1 pinch / 1g. (recommended)
Cardamom 1 pinch / 0,5g. (recommended)
Parsley 2 table spoons / 6g. (recommended)

Cooking instructions:
Add the olive oil to a pan, sauté the chestnuts, sprinkle with the curry, add the lentils and season with vegetable stock, add a little white wine, mix in the curcuma, simmer for about 20 minutes (until the chestnuts are tender). Then puree the soup.
Taste with a pinch of anise, cardamom and herbal salt. At the end, sprinkle finely chopped parsley over it.

9.20 Mung bean stew

Relieves excessive thirst, supports urination, reduces blood lipids, relieves allergies. Strengthens spleen and stomach, strengthens the muscles. Lowers cholesterol, antiparasitic. Stimulates liver function, detoxifying.
Cooking time approx. 2 hours
Calories p. portion: 665
2 portions
Allergens:

Quantity of ingredients:
Mung bean 5/8 lbs - 8oz - 500g / 300g. (yes)
Sunflower oil 2 table spoons / 30g. (recommended)
Amaranth 1/2 teaspoon / 2g. (yes)
Fennel seeds ground 1/2 teaspoon / 2g. (yes)
Cumin (Caraway seed) 1/2 teaspoon / 2g. (yes)
Coriander 1/2 teaspoon / 2g. (yes)
Rice round grain 1/2 cup / 60g. (recommended)
Water 3 cups / 300g. (yes)
Ginger fresh 1 inch / 3g. (recommended)
Kombu seaweed (Saccharina japonica) 1 inch / 2g. (recommended)
Salt 1 pinch / 0,5g. (little)
Parsley 1 table spoon / 3g. (recommended)

Cooking instructions:
Soak mung beans overnight.
Heat sunflower oil in a hot pot. Stir in the amaranth, fennel seeds, cumin and coriander and fry briefly.
admit basmati rice, some ginger and mung beans and roast briefly.
Pour water and heat till it boils.
Add a piece of kombu alga and salt.
Simmer for 1-1/2 hours.
Garnish with parsley or coriander.

9.21 Oyster mushrooms with asparagus

Forces, reduces inflammation, improves digestion, lowers cholesterol, strengthens kidney, stimulates liver function, improves blood circulation, improves medication effect, increases appetite.
Cooking time approx. 30 min
Calories p. portion: 316
4 portions
Allergens: GH

Quantity of ingredients:
Onion white 1 piece / 50g. (yes)
Butter organic 2 table spoons / 40g. (little)
Oyster mushroom 3/4 lbs / 300g. (yes)
Sake 2 table spoons / 40g. (yes)
Parsley 2 table spoons / 40g. (recommended)
Walnuts 2 table spoons / 60g. (yes)
Asparagus (green or white) 1,1 lbs / 500g. (recommended)

Salt 1 pinch / 1g. (little)
Sugar white 1 pinch / 0,1g. (little)
Potato 1 lbs / 500g. (recommended)
Salt (herbal) 1 pinch / 1g. (little)

Cooking instructions:
Cook organically grown potatoes with the skin, otherwise prepare peeled boiled potatoes. Boil the asparagus in salted water with a pinch of sugar and salt. (You can cook an old roll that absorbs the bittering substances.) Slightly sauté the chopped onions in a pan in the butter before frying the oyster mushrooms cut into the same pan. Stew 15 minutes, stirring several times. Add the sake, walnuts and parsley and simmer on low heat while you drain the potatoes and asparagus. Finally, sprinkle some herbal salt over it.
If no fresh asparagus is available, asparagus can be used in jars.

9.22 Porridge with cherries

Strengthens immune system. Improves blood circulation, reduces inflammation, moisturizer dry skin. Little laxative.
Cooking time approx. 10 min
Calories p. portion: 228
2 portions
Allergens: AG

Quantity of ingredients:
Oat flakes (whole grain) 8 table spoons / 60g. (recommended)
Water 1/2 cup / 125g. (yes)
Cow's milk (1.5% fat) 1/2 cup / 125g. (yes)
Salt 1 pinch / 0,2g. (little)
Cream, sweet 30% 2 table spoons / 20g. (little)
Sugar cane sugar 1 table spoon / 8g. (little)
Cherry 1/4 lbs - 4oz (gutted) / 100g. (yes)

Cooking instructions:
Heat water and milk and a pinch of salt till it boils. Sprinkle in 4 tablespoons of coarse rolled oats and cook to a pulp, add 4 tablespoons of fine oatmeal, allow to simmer. Arrange in a preheated bowl and top with cream. Core and add cherries.

9.23 Provencal noodle pan

Improves blood circulation, reduces Inflammation, relieves pain, strengthens the muscles, tendons and bones, diuretic, supports urination.
Cooking time approx. 45 min
Calories p. portion: 196
2 portions
Allergens: ACL

Quantity of ingredients:
Noodles (whole grain) with egg 5/8 oz / 200g. (yes)
Aubergine 1/8 lbs - 2oz / 60g. (yes)
Zucchini 1/8 lbs - 2oz / 60g. (yes)
Peppers 1/8 lbs - 2oz / 50g. (yes)
Beef meat 1/8 lbs - 2oz / 50g. (yes)
Garlic 2 pieces / 4g. (recommended)
Rapeseed oil 1/8 oz / 5g. (yes)
Basic recipe for a vegetable soup 1/4 cup / 60g. (recommended)
Tomato juice 1/3 cup / 75g. (little)
Oregano fresh 1 pinch / 1g. (yes)
Rosemary 1 pinch / 1g. (yes)
Pepper (ground) 1 pinch / 0,5g. (yes)
Salt 1 pinch / 0,5g. (little)

Cooking instructions:
Boil noodles in plenty of salted water, chill and drain.
Wash vegetables, dice aubergine and zucchini.
Core the pepper and cut into cubes of approx. 1 cm.
Braise garlic, minced beef and prepared vegetables in heated oil, pour in vegetable stock and tomato juice and finish cooking.
Add pasta to the sauce.
Heat the whole and season with the spices and salt.

9.24 Pumpkin dumplings with tomato and parsley sauce

Protects the digestive system. Good to fight loss of appetite, flatulence, calms nerves and stomach, helps to digest fat, reduces blood pressure, stimulates liver function, dissolves stagnation.
Cooking time approx. 30 min
Calories p. portion: 380

2 portions
Allergens: ACG

Quantity of ingredients:
Hokkaido pumpkin 1/4 lbs - 4oz / 100g. (recommended)
Chicken egg 2 pieces / 120g. (yes)
Wheat flour 1/2-1/3 cup / 120g. (yes)
Salt 1 pinch / 1g. (little)
Pepper (ground) 1 pinch / 0,5g. (yes)
Nutmeg 1 pinch / 0,2g. (yes)
Lemon peel 1/2 teaspoon / 2g. (yes)
Parmesan 2 table spoons / 20g. (little)
Onion (spring onion) 2 pieces / 40g. (recommended)
Tomato 1/4 lbs - 4oz / 100g. (recommended)
Parsley 1/2 bunch / 50g. (recommended)
Salt 1 pinch / 1g. (little)

Cooking instructions:
Peel the pumpkin with a sharp knife, remove the seeds and cut the pulp
into large cubes. Wrap pumpkin in aluminum foil, bake in preheated
oven at 200°C/392°F for 20 minutes. Pour off any spilled pumpkin juice.
Finely crush the pumpkin with the fork. Stir pumpkin and egg until
smooth. Stir in so much flour until a dough is formed, from which
dumplings can be cut off. Season the mixture with lemon zest, salt,
pepper and nutmeg.
Cut off small dumplings with a teaspoon. Leave pumpkin dumplings in
boiling salted water for approx. 7 minutes.

Roast the onion in a frying pan until lightly fry the tomato cubes, salt
and the chopped parsley.

Arrange pumpkin dumplings in portions with the tomato parsley sauce.
Parmesan to hand.

9.25 Quinoa with peach

Supports erythrocyte production, relieves fatigue, relaxes. Good to fight
gastrointestinal complaints. Relieves pain, detoxifying, bactericide.
Cooking time approx. 20 min
Calories p. portion: 248
2 portions
Allergens:

Quantity of ingredients:
Quinoa 1 cup / 100g. (yes)
Water 1 1/2 cups / 240g. (yes)
Honey 2 teaspoons / 4g. (little)
Peaches 2 pieces / 240g. (yes)
Linseed oil 2 teaspoons / 4g. (recommended)
Lemon Balm (fresh) 1 teaspoon (chopped) / 1g. (yes)
Cinnamon ground 1 pinch / 0,2g. (yes)
Vanilla 1 pinch / 0,2g. (yes)

Cooking instructions:
In the evening: Put quinoa in hot water and boil soft, covered 15 to 20 minutes.
In the morning: Warm up quinoa with 1 tablespoon water.
Steam lightly Peaches in a saucepan or add them fresh. Decorate with fresh lemon balm.
Summer: nectarines, apricots
Winter: Pickled fruit, pear, apples

9.26 Radish with horseradish

Stimulates liver function, detoxifying. Promotes digestion, improves blood circulation, supports urination, reduces thirst.
Cooking time approx. 30 min
Calories p. portion: 196
2 portions
Allergens: GNO

Quantity of ingredients:
Butter organic 1 table spoon / 8g. (little)
Radish (white, green, purple-red) 1/2 piece / 50g. (yes)
Water 2 table spoons / 10g. (yes)
Lemon juice 2 table spoons / 20g. (yes)
White wine 2 table spoons / 20g. (little)
Pepper powder (hot) 1 pinch / 0,2g. (yes)
Sesame oil 1 teaspoon / 3g. (recommended)
Radish horseradish 2 table spoons / 20g. (yes)
Salt 1 pinch / 0,5g. (little)
Parsley 1 Bunch (chopped) / 80g. (recommended)
Rice long grain rice 1/2 cup / 60g. (recommended)
Water 3 cups / 300g. (yes)
Salt 1 pinch / 0,5g. (little)

Cooking instructions:
In a hot pan melt the butter, sautéed into stripes cut radish. Add cold water, lemon juice, white wine, a pinch of rose paprika and stir in the sesame oil; with 2 - 3 tablespoons fresh grated horseradish (alternatively 1 teaspoon from the glass), salt to taste; Sprinkle with chopped parsley.

Place the rice with the water, salt and cook for about 15 minutes.

9.27 Radish juice

Promotes digestion, detoxifying (for example alcohol poisoning), improves blood circulation, supports urination, reduces thirst, prevents cancer, strengthens body cells.
Cooking time approx. 10 min
Calories p. portion: 9
1 portions
Allergens:

Quantity of ingredients:
Radish (white, green, purple-red) 1/2 piece / 50g. (yes)
Water 1 cup / 120g. (yes)

Cooking instructions:
Make the radish juice with the juicer or buy it at the food store.
The fresh press juice is extracted from the root.
For healing purposes one prefers the black radish because of its sharpness.
The pungent taste is due to the mustard oils in the radish juice.
They stimulate bile-juice production in the liver. This has two different effects in our body. The appetite and digestion are promoted and alleviates bile and liver disease.
Drink in small sips.

9.28 Reissue soup with fresh fruits

Diuretic, warming the body from the inside, expands blood vessels, strengthens the muscles, regulates internal organs functions.
Cooking time approx. 1 1/2 hours
Calories p. portion: 143
4 portions
Allergens: G

Quantity of ingredients:
Rice wild (nature rice) 1 cup / 100g. (recommended)
Water 8 cups / 900g. (yes)
Apple (sweet) 1 1/2 cups / 200g. (little)
Butter organic 1 table spoon / 10g. (little)
Vanilla 1 pinch / 0,2g. (yes)
Sugar cane sugar 2 teaspoons / 6g. (little)

Cooking instructions:
Prepare rice congee according to basic recipe.

At the end, add finely chopped fruits to the season, vanilla, chili and butter; sweet to taste.

Variant: With nuts, the dish can always be made richer and more filling.

Effect: Cooked or steamed fruits are easier to digest and act better than raw. For some fruits, which are particularly suitable for hot summer days - such as melons and berries - it is still advisable to add the fruits only to a hot porridge.
Other types of fruit - such as apples, pears, plums and cherries - can also be simmered for a while.

9.29 Ribbon noodles with leaf spinach

Promotes digestion, improves blood circulation, forcing spleen and intestine, improves pancreatic function, Good to fight loss of appetite, flatulence, inflammatory bowel disease, obesity, stomach ulcers, stomach cramps, rheumatism, heartburn, twelffinger intestinal ulcers.
Cooking time approx. 45 min
Calories p. portion: 722
2 portions
Allergens: ACG

Quantity of ingredients:
Spinach 5/8 lbs - 8oz / 250g. (recommended)
Salt 1 pinch / 1g. (little)
Noodles (wheat, ribbon noodles) with egg 5/8 oz / 200g. (recommended)
Olive oil 1 table spoon / 15g. (recommended)
Onion (spring onion) 1 piece / 20g. (recommended)

Cream, sweet 30% 1/2 cup / 100g. (little)
Créme fraiche cheese 1/2 teaspoon / 6g. (little)
Thyme dried 1/2 teaspoon / 2g. (yes)
Basil (fresh) 1/2 teaspoon / 2g. (yes)
Oregano dried 1/2 teaspoon / 2g. (yes)
Nutmeg 1 pinch / 0,5g. (yes)
Pepper (ground) 1 pinch / 0,5g. (yes)
Parmesan 1/2 oz / 20g. (little)
Pine nuts 1 table spoon / 15g. (yes)
Black caraway 1 pinch / 1g. (yes)

Cooking instructions:
Put the dripping wet spinach together with a little salt for 3 minutes ina pot, then drain in a sieve. Then finely cut.

Boil tagliatelle in plenty of salted water.

Heat the oil in a skillet and fry the spring onions rings. Add cream, crème fraiche, thyme, basil, oregano and nutmeg. Stir in the sauce while stirring. Add the spinach, heat briefly, season with nutmeg, salt and pepper.
Drain pasta and mix with the spinach. Season with salt and pepper.
Portion noodles and serve with parmesan and pine nuts. Sprinkle the black cumin over it.

9.30 Rice soup with grated carrots and fresh herbs

Diuretic, warming the body from the inside, expands blood vessels, strengthens the muscles, regulates internal organs functions, reduces blood pressure, strengthens immune system, prevents cancer, reduces radiation damage. Promotes digestion.
Cooking time approx. 5 min
Calories p. portion: 131
4 portions
Allergens: EG

Quantity of ingredients:
Rice wild (nature rice) 1 cup / 100g. (recommended)
Water 6 cups / 700g. (yes)
Carrot 1 piece / 100g. (recommended)

Soy sauce 1 dash / 2g. (yes)
Butter organic 1 teaspoon / 3g. (little)
Ground 1 pinch / 0,3g. (yes)
Curcuma 1 pinch / 0,2g. (recommended)
Herbs various 1 teaspoon (chopped) / 3g. (yes)

Cooking instructions:
In a portion of rice congee according to basic recipe, softly cook a grated carrot, add butter and soy sauce.
Sprinkle with fresh herbs.

Spices and herbs: black cumin, turmeric, cardamom, parsley, sage, thyme, basil, rosemary.

Winter: parsnip, celery, onion, leek, pumpkin
Summer: tomatoes, zucchini, spring onion, radishes, arugula.

9.31 Roasted millet with plum compote

Supports urination, promotes spleen and kidney, strengthens the defense. Good to fight fungi infections.
Cooking time approx. 30 min
Calories p. portion: 139
4 portions
Allergens:

Quantity of ingredients:
Millet 1 cup / 120g. (yes)
Water 1 1/2 cups / 250g. (yes)
Plum 1 1/2 cups / 250g. (yes)
Vanilla pod 1 pinch / 1g. (yes)
Water 5/8 lbs - 8oz / 250g. (yes)
Cinnamon ground 1 pinch / 1g. (yes)
Acerola fruit nectar or powder 1/2 teaspoon / 1g. (little)

Cooking instructions:
Roast millet briefly, pour over water, heat till it boils and let stand for 20 min. to swell.

Cook plums with water, vanilla and cinnamon 10 min. then strain. Add acerola and add to the millet.

9.32 Rosemary Potatoes

Reduces Inflammation, improves digestion, regenerates skin, supports urination, lowers cholesterol. Rosemary stimulates digestion, strengthens lung, promotes spleen and kidney, dries out.
Cooking time approx. 30 min
Calories p. portion: 188
2 portions
Allergens:

Quantity of ingredients:
Potato 6-8 pieces / 420g. (recommended)
Salt (herbal) 1 pinch / 1g. (little)
Olive oil 1 table spoon / 10g. (recommended)
Rosemary 1 teaspoon / 2g. (yes)

Cooking instructions:
Cut the potatoes into half´s, apply a little olive oil on the cut surface, then salt, sprinkle 2 - 3 rosemary needles on the potatoes.
Place the potatoes on the baking tray and bake them in the preheated oven for approx. 25 minutes to 190°C/374°F.

9.33 Semolina dumpling soup

Reduces blood pressure, strengthens immune system, prevents cancer, reduces radiation damage, dissolves stagnation, promotes weight loss. Good to fight immunodeficiency, loss of appetite, flatulence, high blood pressure, depressions, diabetes, diarrhea.
Cooking time approx. 1 hour
Calories p. portion: 287
3 portions
Allergens: ACGLO

Quantity of ingredients:
Butter organic 1/8 lbs - 2oz / 40g. (little)
Chicken egg 1 piece / 65g. (yes)
Salt 1 pinch / 1g. (little)
Pepper (ground) 1 pinch / 0,5g. (yes)
Nutmeg 1 pinch / 1g. (yes)
Wheat semolina 3 oz / 80g. (yes)
Basic recipe for a beef soup (warming) 2 cup / 500g. (recommended)
Parsley 1 table spoon / 10g. (recommended)
Chives 1 table spoon / 10g. (yes)

Cooking instructions:
Knead the ingredients for the dumplings to a firm dough and allow to swell for 30 minutes. Heat the broth (basic recipe for a beef broth warming). Then cut out with a spoon dumplings, place in the prepared broth and let stand for 20 minutes. Before serving, chop parsley and sprinkle with thinly sliced chives.

9.34 Spelled-grid porridge with berries of the season

Little laxative, strengthens immune system, activated cell metabolism, reduces inflammation. Has a stabilizing effect on the blood circulation, good to fight blood circulation disorders.
Cooking time approx. 15 min
Calories p. portion: 244
2 portions
Allergens: AGH

Quantity of ingredients:
Cow's milk (1.5% fat) 1/2 cup / 125g. (yes)
Water 1/2 cup / 125g. (yes)
Spelled semolina 5 table spoons / 50g. (recommended)
Butter organic 2 teaspoons / 20g. (little)
Berries of the season 1/4 lbs - 4oz / 100g. (yes)
Honey 1-2 teaspoons / 5g. (little)
Almond 1-2 teaspoons / 5g. (yes)
Peppermint 3-4 leaves / 2g. (yes)
Cinnamon ground 1 pinch / 0,5g. (yes)
Vanilla 1 pinch / 0,2g. (yes)
Cocoa 1 pinch / 0,5g. (yes)
Coconut grated 1 table spoon / 10g. (little)

Cooking instructions:
Stir in spelled semolina in cold water and boil slowly over medium heat. After boiling, remove from the heat and let simmer for a few minutes. Depending on the desired consistency, some water may have to be added. Stir in the butter and fine grated nuts in the mash and raspberries. Serve with honey or whole-grain sugar as desired.
Spices and aromas: fresh mint, cinnamon or vanilla, cocoa, coconut

Summer: raspberries, blueberries, strawberries

9.35 Supplementary nutrition

Protein-rich drink with very high energy density. Optimized protein content balances nitrogen losses and promotes protein anabolism.
Cooking time approx. 5 min
Calories p. portion: 1045
1 portions
Allergens:

Quantity of ingredients:
Supplementary nutrition 1 package / 250g. (yes)

Cooking instructions:
Use only as directed by the physician or therapist.

9.36 Tea from celery sticks

Mineral and vitamin rich, forces metabolism and dehydrating effect.
Cooking time approx. 15 min
Calories p. portion: 1
4 portions
Allergens: L

Quantity of ingredients:
Celery sticks 2 table spoons (chopped) / 18g. (recommended)
Water 2 cup / 500g. (yes)

Cooking instructions:
Heat the water till it boils and put it aside. Add cutted celery and cook for 10 min. to let go. Strain. Sweet to taste with honey.

9.37 Tea from rose hip

Regulates digestion, improves blood circulation.
Cooking time approx. 10 min
Calories p. portion: 2
4 portions
Allergens:

Quantity of ingredients:
Rose hip tea 2 table spoons / 4g. (yes)
Water 2 cup / 500g. (yes)

Cooking instructions:
Heat the water till it boils and put it aside. Add rosehip and leave for 10 min. to let go. Sweet to taste with honey. Strain when pouring.

9.38 Tea mixture appetizing

Ginger powder is warming, promotes sweating, dissolves stagnation.
Cooking time approx. 10 min
Calories p. portion: 0
4 portions
Allergens:

Quantity of ingredients:
Bitter orange peel 1 teaspoons / 3g. (yes)
Yarrow tea 1 teaspoons / 3g. (yes)
Ginger powder 1g. Or 0,034oz / 1g. (yes)
Horehound leaves 1 teaspoons / 3g. (yes)
Water 2 cups / 500g. (yes)

Cooking instructions:
Brew one tablespoon of tea mixture with half a liter of water and leave for 10 min. to let go. Then strain and drink in small sips before eating.

9.39 Whole milk cereal mash

Reduces Inflammation, antiallergic, has a stabilizing effect on the blood circulation, lowers blood glucose and cholesterol.
Cooking time approx. 20 min
Calories p. portion: 205
1 portions
Allergens: AG

Quantity of ingredients:
Cow's milk (whole milk 3.5% fat) 3/4 cup - 6 oz / 200g. (little)
Water 1/4 cup / 50g. (yes)
Spelled flakes 1/2 oz / 20g. (yes)
Fruit mix juice 1/2 oz / 20g. (little)

Cooking instructions:
Boil the milk with the wholegrain flakes and let it swell. Add the pureed fruit.

Switch between wheat, oats and wholemeal spelled flakes, as well as the fruits. So you get a variety of flavors.

9.40 Yogurt with honey and nuts

Relieves pain, detoxifying, promotes wound healing. Good to fight acute or chronic constipation of the intestine. Dissolves stones.
Cooking time approx. 5 min
Calories p. portion: 258
1 portions
Allergens: GH

Quantity of ingredients:
Yogurt (natural, 3.5% fat) 1/4 lbs - 4oz / 125g. (little)
Honey 2 table spoons / 30g. (little)
Walnuts 1 table spoon / 12g. (yes)

Cooking instructions:
Mix yoghurt with honey and finely chopped nuts.

9.41 Zucchini with basil pesto

Good to fight bloating and nausea. Relaxing and reassuring, promotes digestion, forcing spleen and digestive system, detoxifying, strengthens the muscles and bones, diuretic, supports urination, dissolves stagnation.
Cooking time approx. 25 min
Calories p. portion: 468
3 portions
Allergens: ACGHL

Quantity of ingredients:
Basil (fresh) 1 Bunch / 125g. (yes)
Olive oil 1 table spoon / 20g. (recommended)
Almond 1 table spoon / 15g. (yes)
Parmesan 1 oz / 30g. (little)
Basic recipe for a vegetable soup 2 table spoons / 45g.
(recommended)
Lemon peel 1 teaspoon / 3g. (yes)
Lemon 1 teaspoon / 3g. (yes)
Oregano dried 2 teaspoons / 15g. (yes)

Ground 1 pinch / 1g. (yes)
Salt 1 pinch / 1g. (little)
Pepper (ground) 1 pinch / 1g. (yes)
Noodles (wheat, spaghetti) with egg 5/8 oz / 200g. (recommended)
Salt 1 pinch / 1g. (little)
Olive oil 1 table spoon / 15g. (recommended)
Onion (spring onion) 2 pieces / 40g. (recommended)
Zucchini 5/8 lbs - 8oz / 250g. (yes)

Cooking instructions:
Mix Basil, olive oil, grated almonds, parmesan, vegetable broth and grated lemon peel to a smooth cream puree. Season the pesto with salt, oregano, cumin and pepper.

Boil the spaghetti with a little salt in plenty of water.

Heat the olive oil in a pan and fry the spring onions while stirring. Add zucchini and fry briefly with stirring. The zucchini should be soft with a bite. Season the zucchini with salt.

In a bowl, mix well-drained spaghetti with zucchini and pesto. Season the spaghetti with salt and pepper.

Recommended for dysphagia, loss of appetite, potassium and magnesium requirements.

10 Effects of food

10.1 Use ingredients: recommendable

Acai powder
Adzuki beans
Anise (Common Fennel)
Artichoke
Asparagus (green or white)
Barley flour
Barley grouts
Barley not peeled
Basic recipe for a beef soup (warming)
Basic recipe for a chicken soup (warming)
Basic recipe for a fish soup
Basic recipe for a rice soup (Congee)
Basic recipe for a vegetable soup (nutritious)
Bitter Herb liqueur
Black beans
Blackberry dried (unripe fruit)
Black-eyed peas
Blueberry
Bocksdorn fruits (Fructus Lycii, Goji, goji berry dried
Bread with carob kernel flour
Broad beans (thick beans)
Broccoli
Buckwheat (roasted) Kasha
Buckwheat whole grain
Bulgur (cereals)
Cardamom
Carrot
Carrot (Early Carrot)
Carrot juice without sugar
Celery root
Celery sticks
Chestnut puree
Chestnuts
Codfish
Coffee
Corn (fast polenta)
Corn Grease (Polenta)
Couscous
Cream 10% coffee cream
Crispbread
Crucian
Curcuma
Currant (black)
Curry
Dulse (seaweed)
Fox nut, gorgon nut, makhana

Freshwater fish
Garlic
Ginger fresh
Ginseng root
Green spelt
Ground caraway
Halibut (Flatfish)
Hibiscus
Hokkaido pumpkin
Kidney beans (red)
Kombu seaweed (Saccharina japonica)
Kudzu
Kumquats
Lily bulbs
Linseed oil
Millet flakes
Miso
Miso black (fermented)
Noodles (wheat) with egg
Noodles (wheat, lasagne) with egg
Noodles (wheat, ribbon noodles) with egg
Noodles (wheat, spaghetti) with egg
Oat flakes (whole grain)
Oat fusion (baby food)
Olive oil
Onion (shallot)
Onion (spring onion)
Parsley
Parsley root
Pearl barley
Pearl barley
Perch
Plaice
Potato
Potato (mealy)
Potato flour
Pumpernickel (dark bread)
Pumpkin
Red berry (without sugar)
Rice Basmati
Rice flour
Rice long grain rice
Rice noodles
Rice round grain
Rice variety any
Rice wild (nature rice)
Rosefish
Rusk

Sago (cereals)
Salsify
Savory
Sea buckthorn
Sesame oil
Sesame oil roasted
Soy flour
Soy noodles
Soya Cuisine (soy cream)
Soybean oil
Soybeans
Soybeans, blacks, fermented
Soybeans, yellow
Spelled (Dark) bread
Spelled semolina
Spelled wholemeal flour
Spinach

Stevia (candyleaf, sweetleaf)
Sugar substitute (sweetener)
Sunflower oil
Sweet potato
Thyme
Toast bread (whole grain)
Tomato
Tomato dried
Tomato paste
Topinambur
Trout
Tsampa (roasted barley flour)
Turmeric (yellow root)
Turnips
Wakame
Wheat semolina for children
Whitefish

10.2 Use ingredients: yes

Agar agar (kelp)
Agrimony
Almond
Almond milk
Almond puree
Amaranth
Amaranth Pops
Anchovy / Sardine
Angelica root
Apple (sour)
Apricot
Arrowroot
Aubergine
Avocado
Baking powder
Balm
Bamboo shoots
Banchatee (green tea)
barberry
Barley
Barley grass powder
Barley malt
Basic recipe for a beef soup
Basic recipe for a duck soup
Basil
Basil (fresh)
Batavia
Bay leaf
Bean oil
Beans (green, fresh)
Bearberry leaf
Beef fillet
Beef lungs (calf)
Beef meat

Beef meat (calf)
Beef meatbones
Berries of the season
Berry juice
Bitter orange peel
Black caraway
Black fungus mushroom
Black tea
Blackberry leaves
Blackberry´s
Blackthorn (Sloe)
Blue mallow tee
Blueberry dried
Boletus mushroom
Borage
Borage oil
Boxhorn clover seeds
Breadcrumbs (wheat bread, bread roll)
Brussels sprouts
Buckbean
Buckwheat
Burdock root tea
Bush beans
Butter (half fat)
Butter beans white
Buttermilk
Calamari
Camembert
Campari
Cantaloupe
Capers in olive oil
Carambola (Star fruit)
Carob flour, St. john's bread
Carp

Cashews
Cauliflower
Caviar
Cereal coffee
Chamomile
Chamomile tea
Champignon
Channa-Dal
Chanterelle
Chenpi (chinese tangerine bowl)
Cherry
Cherry (sour)
Chervil
Chervil dried
Chicken Blood
Chicken egg
Chicken egg white
Chicken meat
Chicken yolk
Chickpeas
Chickweed
Chicory
Chili (pod or ground)
Chinese cabbage
Chinese pearl barley
Chives
Chlorella (fresh water)
Chocolate (Diabetic)
Chrysanthemum blossom tea
Cinnamon ground
Cinnamon sticks
Clementine
Clementines
Clove
Cocoa
Coconut milk
Cod
Coix (seeds) YiYi Ren
Cola drink (low calorie)
Coriander
Coriander (fresh)
Corn
Corn (roasted)
Corn flour
Corn germ oil
Corn silk tea
Corn starch
Cottage cheese
Cow's milk (1.5% fat)
Crab
Cranberries
Cranberry
Cranberry
Cranberry juice

Cream sour 10%
Creamer
Cress
Cucumber
Cucumber (bitter)
Cucumber (spicy cucumber)
Cumin (Caraway seed)
Curd cheese 20%
Currant (red)
Currant (white)
Curry paste red
Daisy
Dandelion (young plants)
Dandelion juice
Dandelionroots tea
Dashi
Dates red
Deer meat
Deer meat
Deer's Bones
Dill
Dyer's broom herb
Elderberries
Elderberry blossom tee
Endive salad
Evening primrose oil
Fennel
Fennel seeds ground
Fennel tea
Fenugreek (Trigonella foenum-graecum)
Fernet Branca (herbal bitter liqueur)
Feta cheese
Feta cheese
Fig
Fish innards
Fish pieces mixed (fresh water)
Fish remains
Fish sauce
Flounder
Flower pollen
French beans
Fresh cheese
Fresh cheese from soya
Fresh cheese with herbs
Freshwater crab
Fruit tea
Gail plum
Galangal
Garam Masala powder
Gelatin white
Gelee Royal
Gentian root
Gentian root tea

Ginger oil
Ginger powder
Ginkgo fruit
Ginseng
Goat and sheep's blood
Goat and sheep's milk
Goat cheese
Goose blood
Goose egg
Gooseberry
Gourd
Grapefruit (Pomelo)
Grapefruit dried peel
Grapefruit juice
Grapeseed oil
Grass carp
Green tea
Greengage
Ground
Guava
Hawthorn
Hazelnuts
Herbal tea mix
Herbs bitter
Herbs of Provence
Herbs various
Herbs wild
Herring
Hibiscus tea
Hijiki
Hop
Horehound leaves
Horse meat
Hyssop
Iceberg lettuce
Jasmine blossoms tee
Jellyfish
Juniper berry
Kaki plum
Kalmus
Kefir
King Solomon's-seal
Kiwi
Kohlrabi
Kukicha tea
Lamb bones
Lamb meat
Lamb shoulder
Lamb's lettuce
Lamb's lettuce
Lavender blossoms
Leaf salads (bitter)
Leek
Lemon

Lemon Balm (dried)
Lemon Balm (fresh)
Lemon juice
Lemon peel
Lemongrass
Lentils
Lentils black
Lentils red
Lentils yellow
Lettuce
Licorice root tea
Lima beans
Lime
Lime blossom tea
Linseed
Linseed (crushed)
Liver smoothing tea
Lobster
Longane
Loquate / Japanese medlar
Lotus roots
Lotus seeds
Lovage
Lovage seeds
Luo Han Guo fruit
Lychee
Lychee in Preserved
Mackerel
Mallow (Malva sylvestris) blossom tea
Malt
Mango
Manioc flour
Mare's milk
Marjoram
Martini
Mediterranean fish (cod, plaice,
haddock, sea eel, mackerel)
Medlar
Millet
Mineral water
Mirabelle plum
Miso paste (soy bean paste)
Mixed Pickles
Morel (black, dried)
Morel, dried
Mozzarella
Mu Erh Mushroom
Muesli
Mulled Wine Spice
Mullet
Multi-grain bread (gray bread)
Mung bean
Mung bean sprouting
Mussels

Mustard
Mustard Dijon
Mustard medium hot
Mustard seeds
Mustard sweet
Mutton
Nasturtium (nose-twister or nose-tweaker)
Nectarine
Nettles
Noodles (whole grain) with egg
Nori, purple seaweed, red algae
Nutmeg
Oat
Oat flakes roasted
Oat flour
Oat meal
Oat milk
Octopus
Octopus
Okra
Olives
Olives green
Onion read
Onion white
Orange
Orange blossom
Orange dried peel
Orange grated peel
Orange peel
Oregano dried
Oregano fresh
Oyster mushroom
Oyster shell powder
Oysters
Palm oil
Papaya
Parsnip
Passion blossoms tea
Passion fruit
Peaches
Peaches (canned)
Peanut oil
Peanuts
Pear
Peas
Peas, green
Pepper (ground)
Pepper Cayenne
Pepper powder (hot)
Pepper white (ground)
Peppercorns
Peppermint
Peppermint tea

Pepperoni
Pepperoni, red, pitted, halved
Pepperoni, yellow, pitted, halved
Peppers
Peppers (rose peppers)
Peppers (sweet)
Peppers powder
Pheasant
Pickle
Pig blood
Pigeon
Pigeon egg
Pimento
Pine nuts
Pineapple
Pineapple juice without sugar
Pinto beans speckled
Pistachios
Plum
Plums
Pomegranate
Poppy
Pork ham
Pork ham cooked
Pork ham smoked
Pork knuckle
Pork lung
Pork meat
Pork skin
Prickly pear
Processed cheese 12%
Psyllium seed
Pudding powder vanilla
Pumpkin seed oil
Pumpkin seeds
Quince
Quinoa
Rabbit
Rabbit (wild)
Rabbit meat
Radicchio
Radish
Radish (white, green, purple-red)
Radish black
Radish horseradish
Radish leaves
Rapeseed oil
Raspberry
Raspberry leaf tea
Red beet
Red wine
Reishi mushroom
Rhubarb
Ribworttea

Rice (fragrance)
Rice (Gaoliang / Sorghum)
Rice (whole grain)
Rice black
Rice malt
Rice mash
Rice red
Rice starch
Rice sticky
Romaine lettuce / lettuce salad
Rose blossom tea
Rose hip
Rose hip tea
Rose leaf tea
Rosemary
Rucola
Rye
Rye flour
Rye wholemeal bread
Safflower (Dyer's thistle / Hong Hua)
Saffron
Sage
Sake
Salmon
Sauerkraut (cutted cabbage fermented)
Savoy cabbage / kale
Sea cucumber
Seacrab
Sesame paste (Tahini)
Sesame, black
Sesame, white
Shark
Sheep's milk
Sheep's milk yoghurt
Shiitake, dried
Shrimp
Shrimps
Skim milk powder
Slug
Sorrel
Sour cherries
Sour milk
Sour milk cheese 20%
Sourdough
Soy sauce
Soy Tofu
Soy Tofu smoked
Soybean milk
Soybeans, black
Spelled flakes
Spelled grain
Spiny lobsters
Spurdog (spiny dogfish, Schillerlocken)
St. Benedict's thistle, blessed thistle,

holy thistle, spotted thistle
Star anise
Strawberries
Sugar fructose - fruit sugar
Sugar glucose - grapes sugar
Sugar Milk Sugar
Sunflower seeds
Supplementary nutrition
Tabasco
Tangerine
Tarragon (Estragon)
Tea mixture uric acid lowering
Thistle oil
Thyme dried
Tomato puree
Trout (smoked)
Truffle
Tuna
Turkey breast meat
Turkey ham
Turnip
Umeboshi paste
Umeboshi plums (Japanese apricots)
Valerian
Vanilla
Vanilla pod
Vanilla powder
Vegetable juice
Vinegar (Apple vinegar)
Vinegar (Red wine vinegar)
Vinegar Aceto Balsamico
Vinegar Aceto Balsamico white
Walnut oil
Walnuts
Water
Water hot
Watermelon
Wax gourd
Wheat
Wheat bran
Wheat bulgur
Wheat flatbread/pita bread
Wheat flour
Wheat flour whole grain
Wheat germ oil
Wheat semolina
Wheat/Rye/Gray-black bread with yeast
Wheatgrass juice
Wheatgrass powder
Whey
White beans
White cabbage
Whole grain bread
Wholemeal flour

Wild boar meat
Wild garlic (garlic spinach)
Wild herbs
Wild strawberries
Wormwood herb
Yam root, yam root tuber
Yarrow

Yarrow tea
Yeast
Yew nut
Yoghurt vanilla
Yogi tea
Yogurt (natural, 1.5% fat)
Zucchini

10.3 Use ingredients: little

Acerola fruit nectar or powder
Agave nectar
Almond marzipan
Aloe juice
Apple (sweet)
Apple juice (natural cloudy)
Apple puree
Apricot dried
Apricot jam
Apricot nectar
Apricots
Apricots juice
Banana
Banana (cooking banana)
Beef heart
Beef heart (calf)
Beef kidney
Beef liver
Beef Oxtail pieces
Beef soup meat
Beef stomach
Beer (alcohol-free)
Beer (alcohol-reduced)
Beer (Pils)
Beer (Top-fermented German dark
beer)
Bitter Lemon
Bitter liqueur
Blackberry jam
Blueberry jam
Blueberry juice
Brazil nuts
Bread roll
Brie cheese
Brown ale
Butter organic
Chard
Cherry compote
Cherry juice
Chicken heart
Chicken liver
Chicken stomach
Chocolate

Coconut fat
Coconut flakes
Coconut grated
Coconut meat
Cola drink
Compote (fruits of the season)
Cow's milk (whole milk 3.5% fat)
Cranberry jam
Cream (30% fat)
Cream sour 20%
Cream sour 30%
Cream, sweet 30%
Créme fraiche cheese
Curd cheese 40%
Currant jam (black)
Currant jam (red)
Currant juice (black)
Currants (black)
Currants (red)
Dates dried
Deer's kidneys
Duck (heart)
Duck (slaughtered)
Ducks egg
Edam cheese
Eel
Eel smoked
Emmental cheese
Fig dried
Fructose (glucose)
Fruit mix juice
Ginseng liqueur
Goat
Goat and sheep's brain
Goat and sheep's liver
Goat and sheep's stomach
Goose
Goose fat
Goose parts
Gorgonzola
Gouda cheese
Grape juice red
Grape juice white

Grapes red
Grapes white
Honey
Honey wine (Met)
Ladyfingers
Lamb kidneys
Lamb liver
Lychee liqueur
Lye roll
Mango juice
Maple syrup
Margarine
Margarine (diet)
Mascarpone cheese
Mayonnaise 50%
Mulberry fruit
Mutton
Orange jam
Orange juice
Parmesan
Peanut (roasted)
Peanut butter
Pear juice
Pineapple (from a can)
Plum dried
Pork Bacon
Pork brain
Pork heart
Pork kidneys
Pork liver
Pork marrow bones
Pork stomach
Pork/beef sausage (smoked)
Pork's intestine
processed cheese 30%
Prosecco
Puff pastry
Quail

Quail egg
Rabbit liver
Raisins
Raspberry dried (immature)
Raspberry jam
Red cabbage
Rice sweet
Rum
Salt
Salt (herbal)
Sherry (whine)
Sour cream 15% fat
Spirit
Strawberry jam
Strawberry Juice
Sugar - icing sugar
Sugar brown
Sugar candy white
Sugar cane sugar
Sugar molasses
Sugar palm sugar
Sugar white
Tomato juice
Tonic Water
Vanilla sugar natural
Walnuts roasted
Wheat beer
Wheat flakes
White bread (baguette)
White bread (pretzel sticks)
White bread (roll)
White bread (wheat bread)
White breadcrumbs
White dumpling bread (wheat bread cut into chunks)
White wine
Wormwood
Yogurt (natural, 3.5% fat)

10.4 Do not use contra-acting foods

Beef bone marrow
Clarified butter
Cooking oil
Mayonnaise 80%

Mold cheese
Pork fat (lard)
Pork Lard
Pork sausage (Bratwurst)

11 Herbs and their effects

11.1 Basil (fresh)

It has a beneficial effect on flatulence and nausea, relaxing and soothing.

Good to fight emphysema, bronchitis, whooping cough, high blood pressure, headache, mouth odor, warts, hiccup, gout, migraine.

11.2 Coriander

The essential oils are appetizing, digestive, cramping and soothing in stomach and intestinal disorders.

11.3 Herbs various

Appetizing, lots of trace elements and vitamins

11.4 Cress

Diuretic, supports urination. Good to fight dry mouth, inner agitation, sore throat, diabetes, kidney stones, gastrointestinal complaints, lung problems, menstrual cramps or cancer.

11.5 Chives

Bactericide, prevents cancer, strengthens gastric juice production, promotes digestion and blood circulation, promotes growth, triggers stagnation.

11.6 Oregano fresh

It has an anti-digestive, calming and nerve-strengthening effect, helps to fight cramping stomach and intestinal disorders. The ingredient Carvacrol has an anti-inflammatory effect.

11.7 Oregano dried

It has an anti-digestive, calming and nerve-strengthening effect, helps to fight cramping stomach and intestinal disorders. The ingredient Carvacrol has an anti-inflammatory effect.

11.8 Parsley

Stimulates liver function, detoxifies. Forces urinating. Relieves flatulence. Digestive and menstrual stimulating, birth-accelerating, memory-enhancing, blood-purifying, skin-smoothing.

11.9 Peppermint

Relaxes, frees the lungs and the nose (inhale), regulates the cycle.

Stimulates bile flow and bile production, antispasmodic in gastrointestinal disorders, antimicrobial and antiviral.

11.10 Rosemary

Promotes digestion, relieves bloating, strengthens lung, spleen and kidney. Affects the circulation and nerves. Appetizing. Baths help to fight circulatory disorders as well as with gout and rheumatism.

11.11 Black caraway

Detoxifying, immunoregulatory. In addition, the oil should stimulate the formation of bone marrow cells and generally protect body cells from viruses.

11.12 Thyme dried

Disinfecting. It stimulates the blood circulation, increases the appetite and helps to digest fat meat better. Strengthens lungs and spleen (TCM).

11.13 Lemon Balm (fresh)

Stimulating, antibacterial, encouraging, relaxing, antispasmodic, cooling, antipyretic, analgesic, sweat-inducing, virus-inhibiting. Good for colds, fever, flu, cough, bronchitis, asthma, loss of appetite, bloating, heartburn.

12 Basics of Nutrition

The basic principles of nutrition described herein are general recommendations. They are not aimed at a specific form of therapy. Recommendations concerning a therapy have priority.

12.1 Nutrition

Regular meals in a relaxed atmosphere. A warm breakfast is considered a good start into the day.
The main meals ought to be taken for lunch – supper in the early evening. Pay attention to feeling hungry or sated: don't eat too much nor remain hungry is the rule
Prepare the meals freshly from natural, regional products. Frozen, heat-conserved, industrially prepared or foodstuffs cooked in the microwave oven are rejected.
Choice of foodstuffs according to the season: more cooling food in summer, more warming food in winter.
Eat cooked food at least twice a day. Food and drinks ought to be lukewarm, never ice-cold or hot.
Raw vegetables, briefly cooked vegetables, freshly squeezed juices and mineral water are not recommended. Milk and dairy products are only included in the diet if they don't cause problems. Don't use therapeutic recipes over a longer period without consulting your doctor or therapist.

Varied food
Enjoy the diversity of foodstuffs. Characteristics of a balanced nutrition are variety, suitable combination and a balanced quantity of rich and low energy foodstuffs (on one hand avoiding undersupply with essential nutrients and on the other hand to take to many undesirable substances).

A lot of Cereal Products - and Potatoes
Bread, pasta, rice, cereal flakes (best wholemeal) as well as potatoes contain almost no fat, but many vitamins, mineral nutrients, trace elements, roughage and secondary plant substances. These foodstuffs ought to be taken with low-fat side dishes.

Vegetables and Fruit – „Take Five" every day ... 5 portions of vegetables and fruit a day, as fresh as possible, briefly cooked, or maybe one portion as a juice – ideal as a side dish to every meal as well as snack between meals: Thus a lot of vitamins, mineral nutrients as well as roughage and secondary plant substances

Daily milk and dairy products

Milk and Dairy Products every Day, once or twice per Week Fish; meat, sausages as well as eggs moderately. These foodstuffs contain valuable nutrients like calcium in the milk, iodine selenium and omega-3 fat acids in saltwater fish. Meat is favorable due to its high content of disposable iron and the vitamins B1, B6 and B12. Quantities of 300 – 600 g meat and sausage per week are sufficient. Prefer low-fat products, especially in meat- and dairy products.

Low-fat and fatty Foodstuffs
Fat supplies us with essential fat acids and fatty foodstuffs contain also fat-soluble vitamins. Fat is high in energy; therefore much fat in the food may cause overweight, possibly also cancer. Too many saturated fat acids may further a tendency for cardio-vascular diseases in the long term. Prefer vegetable oils and fats (e.g. rapeseed-, olive-, soya-oils and solid fats produced therefrom). Beware of invisible fat in meat- and dairy products, pastry and sweets as well as in fast-food and convenience foods. 70 – 90 g fat per day is sufficient.

Moderately Sugar and Salt
Take sugar and foods/drinks containing various kinds of sugar (e.g. glucose syrup) only occasionally. Use herbs and spices as well as a little salt creatively. Prefer salt containing iodine.

Plenty of Liquids
Water is absolutely essential. Drink 1-2 l liquids every day. Prefer water (with or without gas) and other low-calorie drinks. Alcoholic drinks should not be taken.

Tasty Dishes, carefully cooked
Cook the meals with as low temperatures and as short as possible, using little water and fat – this preserves the original taste, keeps the nutrients intact and prevents the production of harmful compounds.

Take time and enjoy the food
Take your Time and enjoy your Food
Eating consciously helps to eat right. The eye enjoys food, too. It's fun, invites to enjoy varied dishes and stimulates the feeling of satiety.

Watch your Weight and stay in Motion
A balanced diet and a lot of exercise and sport (30 – 60 min/day) are a healthy combination. The right weight furthers well-being and health.
Thermals, directional effectiveness, digestive power
There are various criteria for judging the effectiveness of herbs and

foodstuffs.

The use of certain herbs and ingredients is based on observations of the effects on the body which these foodstuffs, herbs and spices show after having eaten them. The medical science has developed following system: Every ingredient or herb has a directional effectiveness. Furthermore, there are herbs which have a special effect on certain organs.

The basic condition for a healthy metabolism is to obtain sufficient energy from food and that the digestive process doesn't use too much energy. An easily digestible meal makes content and sated, doesn't cause flatulence and fatigue after the meal. The perfect spices increase the healthiness of our meals. Very often, just small doses of herbs and spices will suffice. They are not used to make us sated, but to help our digestive organs to digest the food.

12.2 Recipes

The recipes list the ingredients to be used and the cooking instructions show how the dish is prepared. The list of ingredients shows the concerned quantities as well as the relevance for the therapy. If you find „less than mentioned", try to comply or find an alternative from the „list of recommended foodstuffs". Mostly it shall result just in a small change of taste when you simply avoid this ingredient.

Mild cooking methods: boiling, stewing, poaching, steaming
Strong cooking methods: barbecuing, roasting, frying, smoking
Balanced cooking methods: deep-frying, baking brick
Deep-freezing and warming in the microwave oven should be avoided (denaturalization).

12.3 Foodstuffs

Foodstuffs have an effect on body and soul like medicinal herbs, only a very much milder one. Dietary advice is mainly based on regional foodstuffs. The knowledge about the effects of each foodstuff and the knowledge, when which foodstuff shall be used, is based on the orthodoschool of medicine. Use ecologic-organic products, if possible. As everything should be cooked for a long time due to a better digestability and very rarely eaten raw, the food agrees with everyone.

The classification of the foodstuffs according to their effect on the body is the basis in order to achieve a harmonious status of health.

Dietary advisors do not recommend certain foodstuffs for everyone. The individual diet is tailor-made for the individual constitution.

Buy only fresh and ripe fruit and vegetables. You ought to leave unripe fruit and vegetables and such with brown spots and wilted leaves behind in the market. In this case take deep-frozen goods (never ready-to-serve dishes!). Fruit and vegetables are deep-frozen immediately after harvesting and often contain more vitamins and minerals than the goods from the vegetable shelf. Whereas conserved or tinned goods contain very much less biological substances. Also, salt, sugar and others are mostly added to the latter. Never leave the foodstuffs in the water after washing them to avoid that many vital substances get drowned. Clean salads, fruit and vegetables immediately before serving.

Please make sure of the hygienic processing of foodstuffs. Clean your salads, fruit and vegetables carefully. When cooking with meat, prepare all ingredients first and then process the meat products. Clean the worktop and tools very carefully. Wooden surfaces ought to be treated with a mild disinfectant regularly in order to reduce germination. Store fruit and vegetables separately, if possible. Harvested fruit and vegetables are still alive and emit e.g. ethylene gas, which makes other products ripen and age faster. Keep meat and fish in the closed packaging or store them in the fridge in closed containers.

12.4 Herbs

There are some basic rules for storing medicinal herbs. On principle, herbs must be protected from direct sunlight, humidity and heat.

Containers for the storage of herbs may be glasses, ceramic jars and even plastic containers. However, plastic is a rather unsuitable material and should only be a short-term solution. In case of glass containers, use a dark material.

Medicinal herbs cannot be kept for any long period. The shelf life of herbs is limited. However, it can be prolonged with suitable storage. The place should be dark, rather cool and absolutely dry. A wooden medicine cabinet, placed not directly next to a source of heat, would be ideal. Never buy large quantities of herbs so as not to have to throw them away. Label the container with the name of the herb and the date of harvesting or processing.

13 Other dietic-books

The following syndromes of dietetics, TCM or for a therapy supplement for cancer are available.

Dietetics

E001. Nutrition of the infant - baby food
E002. Nutrition during lactation
E003. Nutrition in old age
E004. Nutrition of children and adolescents
E005. Nutrition of athletes
E006. Light weight
E007. Pregnancy
E008. Full food

Protein and electrolyte - kidneys

E009. (hemodialysis) dialysis treatment
E010. Acute renal failure
E011. Chronic renal insufficiency
E012. Nephrotic syndrome
E013. Kidney stones (nephrolithiasis)

Gastrointestinal tract - pancreas

E014. Acute pancreatitis (inflammation of the pancreas)
E015. Chronic pancreatitis (inflammation of the pancreas)

Gastrointestinal tract - small intestine and large intestine

E016. Acute obstipation (constipation)
E017. Chronic obstipation (constipation)
E018. Colon irritabile
E019. Diverticulitis
E020. Acquired lactose intolerance (lactose malabsorption)
E021. Fructose malabsorption
E022. Glutensensitive enteropathy (celiac disease)
E023. Colectomy
E024. Short Bowel Syndrome

Gastrointestinal tract - liver, gallbladder, bile ducts

E025. Acute and chronic hepatitis (inflammation of the liver)
E026. Cholelithiasis (bile stones)
E027. fatty liver
E028. cirrhosis

Gastrointestinal tract - Stomach and duodenal intestine

E029. Acute gastritis
E030. Chronic gastritis
E031. Stomach bleeding
E032. Ulcus ventriculi and duodenal ulcer
E033. Condition after gastric surgery

Gastrointestinal tract - oral cavity and esophagus

E034. Stomatitis
E035. Esophageal carcinoma (esophageal cancer)
E036. Refluosophagitis (heartburn)

Special diseases
E037. Phenylketonuria (PKU)
E038. Rheumatic joint diseases

E039. **Metabolism** Obesity (overweight)
E040. Diabetes mellitus
E041. Eating disorders (underweight)

Fat metabolism
E042. Hypercholesterolaemia (increased cholesterol level)
E043. Hepatic Encephalopathy

Heart and circulation
E044. Arteriosclerosis (arterial calcification)
E045. Heart insufficiency
E046. Hypertension
E047. Hyperuricaemia and gout

E048. **Changed nutrient requirements** In case of fever
E049. For malignant diseases
E050. After burns
E051. Radiation and chemotherapy

E100. **CANCER** Pancreatic cancer
E101. Bladder cancer
E102. Blood cancer (leukemia)
E103. Breast cancer
E104. Colorectal cancer
E105. Gastric cancer
E106. Kidney cancer
E107. Esophageal cancer

E200. **TCM** Bladder - moisture heat in the bladder Bladder - moisture and cold in the bladder Bladder - emptiness and cold in the bladder
E201. Large intestine - external cold affects the large intestine Large intestine - moisture heat in the large intestine
E202. Large intestine - heat blocks the intestine II acute
E203. Large intestine - dryness of the colon
E204. Large intestine - Yang deficiency (cold)
E205. Heart - Blood insufficiency
E206. Heart - Blood stagnation
E207. Heart - Fire
E208. Heart - Hot mucus clogs the heart pores
E209. Heart - Cold mucus clogs the heart pores
E210. Heart - Qi deficiency
E211. Heart - Yang deficiency
E212. Heart - Yin deficiency
E213. Liver - Ascending Liver Yang
E214. Liver - Blood deficiency
E215. Liver - Blood stagnation

E216. Liver - Moisture heat in liver and gall bladder Liver - Fire
E217. Liver - Gall bladder Qi-Empty Liver - Cold in the liver meridian
E218. Liver - Qi stagnation Liver - Wind Liver - Wind with ascending liver Yang
E219. Liver - Wind with blood anemic
E220. Liver - Wind with extreme heat
E221. Lung - Qi deficiency Lung - Mucus-moisture in the lungs
E222. Lung - Mucus-heat in the lungs
E223. Lung - Mucus-cold in the lungs
E224. Lung - Dryness of the lungs
E225. Lung - Wind-heat attacks the lungs
E226. Lung - Wind-cold affects the lungs
E227. Lung - Yin deficiency
E228. Stomach - Bloodstagnation Stomach - Fire
E229. Stomach - Cold with liquid
E230. Stomach - Nutrition stagnation
E231. Stomach - Qi deficiency
E232. Stomach - Rebellious Qi
E233. Stomach - Yin Emptiness
E234. Spleen - Heat and moisture attack the spleen
E235. Spleen - Coldness and moisture affects the spleen
E236. Spleen - Qi deficiency
E237. Spleen - Qi deficiency + Declining spleen Qi
E238. Spleen - Qi deficiency + spleen does not control the blood
E239. Spleen - Yang deficiency
E240. Kidney - Heart and kidney no longer communicate
E241. Kidney - Jing deficiency
E242. Kidney - Kidneys cannot receive the Qi
E243. Kidney - Qi is not stable
E244. Kidney - Yang deficiency
E245. Kidney - Yin deficiency

For further information visit di-book.com.